# 100 Swiss Recipes

Lev Well

Copyright © 2015

All rights reserved.

ISBN: 1518893538
ISBN-13: 978-1518893537

# CONTENTS

## Appetizers and Salads ............................................................ 8

   Cheese Salad - Swiss Style ........................................................ 8

   Cocktail Salad - Swiss Style ...................................................... 9

   Dipped SPAM Swiss Sandwiches ............................................. 9

   Ham and Swiss Croissants ....................................................... 10

   Meat Salad - Swiss Style ......................................................... 10

   Simple Sauteed Swiss Chard ................................................... 11

   Swiss Bacon Appetizer ............................................................ 12

   Swiss Flan ................................................................................ 13

   Swiss Fondue #1 ..................................................................... 14

   Swiss Fondue #2 ..................................................................... 15

   Swiss Loaf and Ham ............................................................... 15

   Swiss Meat Loaf ...................................................................... 17

   Swiss Tuna Bunnies ................................................................ 17

   Swiss Wurst Salad ................................................................... 18

## Soups ........................................................................................ 19

   Broccoli and Swiss Cheese Soup ............................................ 19

   Busecca Ticinese ..................................................................... 19

   Cauliflower Swiss Cheese Soup ............................................. 21

Delicous Swiss Wild Garlic Soup ........................................... 22

Lentil Soup with Liver Dumplings ......................................... 23

Soup with Bread and Cheese ................................................. 25

Swiss Cucumber Soup ........................................................... 25

Swiss Gerstensuppe (Barleysoup) ......................................... 26

Swiss Potato Soup .................................................................. 27

Welsh Style Soup ................................................................... 28

White Bean Soup With Swiss Chard ..................................... 29

Hot dishes .................................................................................... 30

Bacon Spinach Swiss Omelet ................................................ 30

Baked Swiss Steak ................................................................. 31

Creole Swiss Steak ................................................................ 32

Crockpot Swiss Steak ............................................................ 32

Swiss Cheese and Crab Pie .................................................... 33

Mushroom and Swiss Patty Melt With Peas ......................... 33

Mushroom-Swiss Hamburger Pie .......................................... 34

Onion Swiss Steak ................................................................. 35

Pressure Cooker Swiss Pepper Steak .................................... 36

Rösti With Papaya Salad ....................................................... 36

Rösti ....................................................................................... 38

Raclette with Shrimps ........................................................... 38

Rostis With Smoked Salmon and Dill Creme ............39

Savory Swiss Steak ............................................40

Spam Swiss Pie ..................................................42

Speedy Swiss Steak ............................................42

Swiss Bacon and Eggs .........................................43

Swiss Chalet Dip .................................................44

Swiss Chard With Cheese ....................................45

Swiss Cheddar Fondue ........................................45

Swiss Cheese and Sausage Deep Dish ..................46

Swiss Cheese Chicken Casserole .........................47

Swiss Cheese Fondue ..........................................48

Swiss Cheese Meat Loaf ......................................48

Swiss Chicken ....................................................49

Swiss Fried Potatoes (Rösti) ................................50

Swiss Omelet Roll ..............................................50

Swiss Parmesan Potato Casserole ........................51

Swiss Roll Rice ..................................................52

Swiss Scrambled Eggs ........................................53

Swiss Sour Cream Casserole ...............................54

Swiss Vegetable Medley ......................................55

Traditional Swiss Raclette ...................56

- Traditional Swiss Raclette .................................................. 57
- Vegan Swiss Fondue ......................................................... 58
- Venison Swiss Steak #1 ..................................................... 59
- Venison Swiss Steak #2 ..................................................... 59

Desserts, Baking and Beverages ................................................ 60

- Baseler Leckerli (Swiss Spice Cookies) ..................................... 60
- Broccoli Onion Swiss Quiche ................................................ 61
- Cheese Pie (Käse Wake) ..................................................... 62
- Chocolate Fondue ........................................................... 63
- Christmas Swiss Roll ....................................................... 64
- Eierochrli (Swiss Carnival Cakes) .......................................... 65
- Garlic Bread ............................................................... 66
- Matcha and mandarin swiss roll ............................................. 67
- Mocha Fondue ............................................................... 68
- Pear Bread ................................................................. 68
- Swiss Almond Macaroons ..................................................... 69
- Swiss Apple Pie ............................................................ 70
- Swiss Cheese and Crab Pie .................................................. 71
- Swiss Cheese Gougere ....................................................... 72
- Swiss Cheese Potato Bread .................................................. 72
- Swiss Chocolate Brownies ................................................... 74

| | |
|---|---|
| Swiss Chocolate Crispies | 75 |
| Swiss Mocha Coffee Mix | 76 |
| Swiss Mocha Mix | 76 |
| Swiss Noodle Bake | 77 |
| Swiss Nut Torte | 78 |
| Swiss Pudding | 79 |

Miscellaneous.....................................................................80

| | |
|---|---|
| Anchovy Sauce | 80 |
| Brandy Sauce #1 | 80 |
| Brandy Sauce #2 | 81 |
| Chili Sauce (For Swiss Steak) | 81 |
| Coffee Butter Sauce | 82 |
| Curry Sauce | 82 |
| Garlic Sauce | 83 |
| Geneva Sauce | 83 |
| Marinade for Meat | 84 |
| Red Beet Sauce | 85 |
| Spinach and Swiss Chard Pasta | 85 |
| Swiss Asparagus Au Gratin - side dish | 86 |
| Swiss Broccoli Pasta | 87 |
| Swiss Sauced Broccoli - side dish | 88 |

Swiss Style Green Beans - site dish......................................88

Tomato Sauce .......................................................................89

## Appetizers and Salads

**Cheese Salad - Swiss Style**

### *Ingredients*

125 g Swiss cheese
1 potato
2 sour apples
1 hard-boiled egg
40 g celery root
30 g nuts
2 1/2 tablespoons mayonnaise
1 tablespoon whipped cream
lemon juice
ground black pepper
salt

### *Instructions*

Dice cheese, apple and egg. Grate celery. Chop nuts. Combine all these products with mayonnaise and cream. Stir and season with lemon juice, pepper and salt.

## Cocktail Salad - Swiss Style

### *Ingredients*

For 1 serving:
25 g cheese
25 g pineapple
20 g cashew
10 g cottage cheese
20 g sour cream
lettuce leaf
salt to taste

### *Instructions*

Dice the cheese and pineapple. Chop the cashew. Layer in a chalice on lettuce leaf the cheese, pineapple and nuts.

Rub the cottage cheese through a sieve. Mix it with sour cream. Season the salad with this mixture.


## Dipped SPAM Swiss Sandwiches

### *Ingredients*

12 ounces spam luncheon meat - cut into 12 slices
6 Swiss cheese slices
12 slices white bread
3 eggs
6 tablespoons milk
3 tablespoons butter or margarine
soft-spread strawberry cream cheese

### *Instructions*

Place spam and cheese on 6 bread slices. Cover with remaining bread slices. Beat together eggs and milk in a shallow bowl. Dip both sides of the sandwich in egg mixture. Grill in the griddle the sandwiches in butter on medium heat until browned and the cheese is melted. Serve with strawberry cream cheese.

Serves 6.

## Ham and Swiss Croissants

### *Ingredients*

3 tablespoon Butter (45mL)
3 cups Mushrooms, sliced (750mL)
3 tablespoon Green onion, sliced (45mL)
1 1/2 tablespoon Flour (25mL)
3/4 cup Milk (175mL)
Salt Pepper 4 lg Croissants, halved
8 slices Ham
6 oz Swiss cheese, sliced (170g)

### *Instructions*

Melt butter in saucepan. Saut mushrooms and onions until tender and mushroom liquid has evaporated. Blend in flour. Gradually stir in milk. Cook and stir over medium heat until mixture comes to a boil and thickens. Add salt and pepper to taste. On bottom half of each croissant layer 2 slices of ham, one quarter of the cheese and one quarter of the mushroom sauce; replace top of croissant. Bake in 350°F (180°C) oven about 15 minutes or until heated through.

## Meat Salad - Swiss Style

## Ingredients

160 g meat boiled
40 g lettuce
40 g onion
60 g salted cucumber - peeled
70 g apples
20 g olive oil
5 g sugar
20 g greens
vinegar
mustard
ground black pepper
salt

## Instructions

Slice boiled meat, lettuce, onion, cucumbers and apples. Combine them in a pan and mix. Season with olive oil, sugar, vinegar, mustard, pepper, salt. Transfer to a salad bowl.

### Simple Sauteed Swiss Chard

## Ingredients

2 bunchs swiss chard, rainbow if possible
2 teaspoons olive oil
1 onion, sliced in rings
2 cloves garlic, chopped coarse
1/2 teaspoon salt
1/8 cup dry sherry wine

## Instructions

1. Clean the chard well. Make sure it's free of any sand and dirt particles. (I fill a large basin with water and wash it in three changes of water.) Don't spin the leaves dry - leave some water clinging to them. You'll need the moisture for cooking.

2. Meanwhile, heat the olive oil in a heavy pot over a medium flame. Sautee the onions for about ten minutes, until they're golden yellow. Add the garlic and sautee for another minute or two, stirring.

3. Add the chard to the pot. Pour in the salt and wine. Cover the pot and cook, stirring every couple of minutes for about ten minutes. You want the chard nicely warmed through and softened, but still bright.

Source: "Foodista.com – The Cooking Encyclopedia Everyone Can Edit".


**Swiss Bacon Appetizer**

## *Ingredients*

6 slices bacon
1 (8 oz.) pkg. crescent rolls
4 slices Swiss cheese
3 eggs, slightly beaten
3/4 cup milk
1 tablespoon instant minced onion
1 tablespoon diced parsley

## *Instructions*

Cook, drain and crumble bacon and set aside. Separate rolls into 4 rectangles and press into 2 well-greased and floured 8-inch square pans. Place 2 cheese slices over dough in each pan. Combine eggs, milk and onion. Pour 1/2 milk mixture over cheese in each pan. Sprinkle 1/2 bacon and parsley over each pan. Bake at 425°F for 15- 18 minutes. Cut into 2-inch squares.

**Swiss Flan**

A Swiss cheese pie is called "flan". The pastry for this pie is sometimes closer to a rich biscuit dough, but in other versions a short pastry may be used. The word "flan" means in Switzerland a cheese custard in pastry. And sometimes Swiss Flan is made with onions and cheese in custard.

## *Ingredients*
1 cup Biscuit mix
3 tablespoons Butter
1/4 cup Light cream

FILLING:
1 Onion, large, sliced or chopped
2 tablespoons Butter
2 Eggs, beaten
2 cups Natural Gruyere cheese (1/2 lb), shredded
1/4 ts Salt

## *Instructions*
PASTRY:
TO MAKE THE PASTRY, chop butter into the biscuit mix, work in cream, and roll out on lightly floured board; or press into a 9 inch pie plate, fluting the edges. Chill while preparing filling.

FOR THE FILLING, cook onion in butter until golden; cool slightly. Add eggs, cheese, and salt. Pour this mixture into pastry, and bake in oven preheated to 425 degrees F. (very hot) for 15 minutes; then reduce heat to 350 degrees F. (moderate) and continue baking 25 to 30 minutes or until a knife inserted in the center comes out clean.

Serve warm as a luncheon entree to 4 to 6 persons, or cut into small wedges for appetizers. Makes 10 to 12 appetizers.

VARIATIONS: Instead of this pastry, regular pie crust may be used. Or make pastry of 1 cup flour, 1 teaspoon baking powder, 1/4 teaspoon salt, 1/3 cup butter, and 1 beaten egg. Do not attempt to roll out this butter-rich pastry; press it with your fingers into pie pan, fluting the edges.

## Swiss Fondue #1

### *Ingredients*

1/2 garlic clove
1 2/3 cups dry white wine
1 pound Gruyere cheese, grated coarse
2 teaspoons cornstarch
1/4 cup Kirsch or more to thin fondue if necessary
Nutmeg to taste
2 loaves crusty French bread, cut in cubes

### *Instructions*

Rub inside of double boiler with the garlic clove, add the wine. Heat until hot and add the cheese by the handful, stirring all the while. When all the cheese is melted, add, while stirring the Kirsch which has been blended with the cornstarch. Add nutmeg and shake of pepper to taste. Keep over hot water or in fondue pot over a low flame. Add Kirsch if fondue gets too thick.

Serves 4 to 6.

Source: "Foodista.com – The Cooking Encyclopedia Everyone Can Edit".

**Swiss Fondue #2**

## *Ingredients*

2 cups dry White Wine
1 Garlic Clove
1 lb Swiss Cheese
3 tablespoons Flour
1 tablespoon Lemon Juice
1/4 teaspoon White Pepper
Salt to taste
Nutmeg to taste

## *Instructions*

Rub the inside of the fondue pot with the garlic clove and add clove to pot. Heat up the white wine and lemon juice on medium low heat - should be hot but do not boil.

Mix Flour and Cheese in a bowl. Slowly add cheese mixture while stirring. Add remainder of ingredients while stirring.

Optional: Add a splash of Kirsch or Blackberry Brandy.

To Dip: Italian bread cut into cubes, vegetables, flat breads.

**Swiss Loaf and Ham**

## *Ingredients*

3 1/2 cups all-purpose flour (3 1/2 to 4 cups)
2 packages Fleischmann's® Rapid Rise Yeast
2 tablespoons sugar
1/4 teaspoon salt
1 cup very warm water (120° to 130°F)
1/4 cup prepared mustard
2 tablespoons butter or margarine - softened
3 cups chopped cooked ham (about 1 pound)
1 cup grated Swiss cheese (4 ounces)
1 4-ounce jar diced pimientos - well drained
3/4 cup diced dill pickles
1 egg - lightly beaten

## *Instructions*

Take a large bowl and combine in it 1 1/2 cups flour, yeast, sugar and salt. Add warm water, mustard and butter and stir. Add enough of the remaining flour and mix to make soft dough. Knead on floured surface until the dough becomes smooth and elastic. Cover; let it rest on floured surface for 10 minutes.

Roll the dough into 10 – 15 inches rectangle. Grease with butter the baking sheet. Place the dough rectangle in the baking sheet. Sprinkle lengthwise over the central third of the dough, with ham, cheese, pimientos and pickles. Make cuts from the filling to the dough edges at 1-inch intervals along the sides of filling. Alternating sides, fold strips at an angle across the filling. Cover. Let it stand for about 20 to 40 minutes in the warm to rise, until almost doubled in size.

Brush the loaf with egg. Bake at 375°F for 35 minutes or until done. Remove from sheet. Serve warm. Refrigerate leftovers; reheat to serve.

Serves 6.

**Swiss Meat Loaf**

*Ingredients*

1 egg
1/2 cup evaporated milk
1/2 teaspoon rubbed sage
1 teaspoon salt
1/2 teaspoon black pepper
1 1/2 pounds lean ground beef
1 cup Ritz cracker crumbs
3/4 cup grated Swiss cheese
1/4 cup finely chopped onion
2-3 strips bacon, cut into 1-inch pieces

*Instructions*

Preheat oven to 350 degrees F.

Beat the egg in a large bowl. Add evaporated milk, sage, salt and pepper, and mix. Add beef, crumbs, 1/2 cup of the cheese and the onion; blend. Form into a loaf and place in a 2-quart rectangular baking dish. Arrange bacon pieces on top of loaf. Bake 40 minutes.

Sprinkle remaining cheese on top and bake 10 minutes longer.

**Swiss Tuna Bunnies**

*Ingredients*

3 ounces Swiss cheese, diced (about 1/2 cup)
1 can tuna, well drained
1/2 cup salad dressing

1 teaspoon lemon juice
2 tablespoons minced onion
1/2 teaspoon salt
4 hamburger buns

## Instructions

Toss all ingredients except hamburger buns lightly until well mixed. Split the buns, spread with butter and then tuna mixture. Wrap individually in foil. Bake about 20 minutes at 300-350°F.

**Swiss Wurst Salad**

## Ingredients

200 g German style sausage, use good quality frankfurters or French cervelas (Lyoner) or Ring Bologna or German Fleischwurst
50 g Swiss or German Emmental cheese
5-6 pickled gherkins (German or Polish variety is best)
1 small onion
olive oil
vinegar
salt
pepper
parsley

## Instructions

1. finely chop up the sausage, cheese, gherkins and the onion
2. put it all into a bowl
3. add some of the liquid of the pickled gherkins, olive oil, a little vinegar, very little salt, pepper and parsley
4. move it all and serve cold, preferably with some German rye bread

Source: "Open Source Food" - opensourcefood.com.

## Soups

**Broccoli and Swiss Cheese Soup**

### Ingredients

2 1/2 lb Broccoli, cut into 1-inch florets
1 cup Chopped leeks or green onion
4 teaspoon Butter
4 tablespoons Flour
4 cups Chicken stock
1 cup Light cream
1 cup Shredded Swiss cheese
1/8 teaspoon Nutmeg

### Instructions

Salt and pepper to taste Cut enough florets to measure 2 cups. Cut rest of broccoli into 1-inch pieces. Cook florets and broccoli pieces, separately, in lightly salted water until just tender. (Florets will be done first). Immediately rinse in cold water. Drain. Set florets aside until serving time. In a large saucepan saute leeks in butter until tender; usually about 4 minutes. Sprinkle in flour and cook one more minute, stirring with whisk. Remove from heat and stir in broth. Return to heat and simmer for 5 minutes, stirring occasionally. Add broccoli pieces to broth and puree in blender in batches, until smooth. Just before serving, blend in cream and Swiss cheese. Simmer gently until cheese melts. Add nutmeg, salt, pepper. Add reserved florets and heat through.

**Busecca Ticinese**

## *Ingredients*

3 tablespoons Borlotti beans
3 carrots
1 leek
1 small celery knob
1 pound honeycomb tripe
1 ounce butter
1 garlic clove - mashed
1 tablespoon tomato paste
5 cups bouillon
1/4 teaspoon caraway seeds
1 thyme sprig
2 3/4 ounces grated parmesan cheese
1 parsley sprig
salt and freshly ground pepper

garlic bread:
7 ounces French bread
1 3/4 ounces butter
4 garlic clove - mashed
1/4 ounce Gruyere cheese - grated
1 tablespoon parsley
salt and freshly ground pepper to taste

## *Instructions*

Soak beans overnight. Drain. Boil in lightly salted water until tender. Drain.

Clean, trim and wash carrots, leek, celery. Slice the leek diagonally. Slice the carrots finely. Slice the celery finely. Cut the celery into squares.

Cut the tripe into strips 1 9/16 inch long and 1/16 inch wide. Pour water in a kettle. Add salt and bring to boil. Add tripe and boil for 2 1/2 hours. Drain.

Preheat butter in a saucepan. Saute vegetables briefly. Add tripe, garlic and tomato paste. Saute. Moisten with bouillon and simmer for 20 minutes. Season with caraway, thyme, salt and pepper. Add Borlotti beans and heat.

Garnish with parsley. Serve in soup plates. You can also sprinkle the soup with cheese.

Prepare Garlic Bread: Cut bread into slices, toast in oven. Beat butter until creamy, chop parsley finely, blend butter with garlic, cheese (Gruyere) and parsley. Salt and pepper to taste. Spread bread with butter mixture, gratinee under broiler until golden brown. Serve with soup.

**Cauliflower Swiss Cheese Soup**

*Ingredients*

1 sweet onion, chopped
2 peeled and sliced carrots
2 sliced celery stalks
1 clove garlic, minced
2 tablespoons olive oil
3 cups chicken broth
1 package frozen cauliflower
1 cup milk
pinch of red pepper

1 teaspoon thyme
2 cups grated Swiss cheese
salt and pepper to taste

## *Instructions*

In pressure cooker over medium heat, add olive oil and saute onions until they begin to soften and turn translucent. Add garlic and saute for 2 minutes more. Add celery, cauliflower, carrots, chicken broth, thyme, and red pepper.

Turn heat to high, seal pressure cooker, and wait until it comes to 15 p.s.i. (When the steam vents continually) Turn down to medium to low (just so steam gently vents) and time for 12 minutes.

Remove from heat and let cool down slowly. Remove cover and using a hand blender, or a regular blender, blend until all vegetables are liquefied.

Return to stove and turn heat to low, and add one cup of milk and swiss cheese. Cook, stirring until milk is incorporated and cheese is fully melted. Salt and pepper to taste.

Garnish with parsley.

Source: http://themerlinmenu.blogspot.com/2009/10/cauliflower-swiss-cheese-soup.html.


**Delicous Swiss Wild Garlic Soup**

## *Ingredients*
50 g leek
0.5 onion
20 g celery

250 g potatoes
100 g wild garlic
50 g butter
8 dl hot chicken bouillon
2 dl cream
salt and pepper
whipped cream

## *Instructions*

Peel all vegetables and cut them into small cubes.

Wash wild garlic and cut into bite-size pieces. If you cannot find wild garlic, use real garlic. Cut it each into four pieces.

Melt the butter and sauté the vegetables but be careful to not let them get brown.

Poor chicken bouillon over the vegetables and cook until they are soft. You may substitute the chicken bouillon with vegetable bouillon to make it a true vegetarian dish.

Add cream and wild garlic to soup and bring to a boil. If you are using real garlic, I suggest cooking it just a bit longer. That way the garlic will be soft and will mash easier. Now take the soup off heat and mash all the ingredients. Now pass it through a sieve. Heat up the soup again.

Taste the soup with salter and pepper.

Stir some whipped cream into soup, quickly mix with a hand mixer.

This soup is now ready to be served. Serve hot.

Source: http://www.bukisa.com/articles/120937_delicous-swiss-wild-garlic-soup.

## Lentil Soup with Liver Dumplings

### *Ingredients*

For Soup:
1 small Onion, finely chopped
30 g Bacon (1 oz), diced
1/4 Leek, diced
20 g Butter (0.75 oz)
80 g Red lentils (2.75 oz)
1 liter Chicken broth (2 pints)
1/2 cup Whipping cream

For Liver Dumplings:
100 g Chicken liver (3.5 oz)
40 g Butter (1.5 oz)
80 g Bread crumbs (2.75 oz)
2 Egg yolks
1 Egg white

### *Instructions*

Sauté the bacon and the onion in the butter. Add the lentils and the leek. Sauté for a moment. Moisten with broth, bring to boil and simmer until the lentils become tender.

Skin the liver mince and press through a fine sieve. Beat the butter until smooth, add the liver and mix well. Stir in egg yolks and bread crumbs. Salt and pepper. Beat the egg white until stiff and fold into liver mixture.

Bring water to simmer in a skillet, add salt. Form dumplings with two teaspoons and boil for 5 minutes. Remove from water and place in a bowl with cold water.

Blend the soup in a blender. Strain through a sieve and return to saucepan. Add the cream and bring to boil. Add the dumplings and reheat.

**Soup with Bread and Cheese**

## *Ingredients*

2 slices of white bread
2 tablespoons butter
1 liter meat stock or water
6-8 tablespoons Swiss cheese chopped
1/2 cup milk
1/2 cup cream
2 tablespoons parsley chopped

To taste:
ground black pepper
salt
caraway

## *Instructions*

Dice bread and fry on butter in a deep pan until golden brown. Add meat stock and simmer on small heat for 10 minutes. Add milk and cream. Remove from heat. Add the cheese, while gently stirring. Salt and pepper to taste. Sprinkle the soup with caraway and serve hot.

## Swiss Cucumber Soup

### *Ingredients*

2 1/2 cups Cucumbers (peeled, seeded and sliced)
1 mediumd Onion (halved and sliced)
4 tablespoons Chopped fresh parsley OR 2 tablespoons Dried parsley
1/4 teaspoon Sea salt
1/2 teaspoon Fresh dill weed OR 1/4 ts -Dried dill
2 tablespoons Corn oil
2 tablespoons Arrowroot or cornstarch
1 3/4 cup Water
2 cup Light soy milk or skim milk
1/4 teaspoon Ground black pepper
6 Sprigs of fresh dill

### *Instructions*

In a large saucepan, saute cucumbers, onion, parsley, salt and dill in oil until vegetables are translucent. In a small bowl, whisk arrowroot with water. Pour into sauted vegetable mixture and stir over medium heat until thickened. Gradually add soy milk and stir until smooth and creamy. Simmer for 3 minutes. Stir in pepper, ladle into serving bowls, garnish with dill and serve hot.

## Swiss Gerstensuppe (Barleysoup)

### *Ingredients*

Soup for cold Switzerland winter

1 tablespoon butter
105 g field garlic, slitted

150 g carrots, diced
170 g celery, diced
100 g bacon bits or Air-dried beef from the Grisons, diced
120 g pearl barley
1 onion
1 veal-tootsie
1.5 liter water
2 tablespoon bouillon
salt
pepper

## *Instructions*

Butter a pan and wait till it's warm.
Add the field garlich, carrots, celery and bacon bits. Steam for 5 minutes.
Add the pearl barley and steam it in short.
Add the water.
Add the bouillon and let it cook. Boil the heat down, cover and let it cook for 30 min.
Take the veal-tootsie out and flavor the soup and serve.

Source: "Open Source Food" - opensourcefood.com.


**Swiss Potato Soup**

## *Ingredients*

4 small potatoes
1/2 onion
1 large flat white turnip
4 tablespoons butter
3 cups boiling water
1/3 cup flour

1 quart scalded milk
1 1/2 teaspoons salt
1/8 teaspoon pepper

## Instructions

Wash, pare, and cut potatoes in halves. Wash, pare, and cut turnips in one-quarter inch slices. Parboil together ten minutes, drain, add onion cut in slices, and three cups boiling water.

Cook until vegetables are soft. Drain, reserving the water to add to vegetables after rubbing them through a sieve. Add milk, reheat, and bind with butter and flour cooked together. Season salt and pepper.

**Welsh Style Soup**

## Ingredients

2 leek stems
1 cauliflower head (about 500 g)
1-2 onions
1-2 tablespoons rice
2 tablespoons short macaroni
2 tablespoons butter
1 tablespoon flour
1 liter water
200 g cheese

To taste:
parsley
celery
ground black pepper
salt

## Instructions

Cut the leek into strips. Cut onions into rings. Divide the cauliflower into florets. Chop the greens: parsley and celery. Boil the prepared vegetables in a pan with 1 liter slightly salted water for 30 minutes.

Pour part of the vegetable broth in another pan. Add rice and macaroni. Boil until readiness. Transfer the pan content to the first pan.

Preheat butter in a frying pan. Add flour and fry until brown. Dilute the flour with broth and pour in the first pan with soup. Season with salt and pepper.

To serve, put in a plate a thin slice of cheese and pour hot soup.

### White Bean Soup With Swiss Chard

## Ingredients

1 1/2 cups dried navy or cannellini beans, soaked overnight
2 tablespoons olive oil
2 medium onions, coarsely chopped
2 carrots, coarsely chopped
2 cloves garlic, crushed
1/2 cup canned tomatoes
2 tablespoons chopped fresh rosemary
2 1/2 qt chicken stock or water
salt and pepper to taste
2 tablespoons butter
1 bunch Swiss chard, rinsed, trimmed and chopped
1 cup Parmesan cheese

## Instructions

In your soup pot, heat the oil and cook the onions and carrots over med heat for about 10 minutes. Add garlic, tomatoes, and rosemary. Cook 1 minute more. Add the drained beans and stock or water. Bring to a boil, then reduce heat and simmer 1 1/2 hours or until beans are very tender. Use a slotted spoon to remove 1 1/2 cup beans from the pot, transfer to a bowl, and use a fork to mash. Return the mashed beans to the soup and continue cooking 20 minutes more. Meanwhile, in a skillet, melt the butter and cook the Swiss chard over high heat, stirring constantly, for 5 minutes. Add salt and paper to taste. Stir the chard into the soup. Serve soup with Parmesan cheese as garnish.

Source: http://tuftscook.wikidot.com/soups:white-bean-soup-with-swiss-chard.

## Hot dishes

**Bacon Spinach Swiss Omelet**

### Ingredients

1 1/2 teaspoons each of butter and peanut oil or vegetable oil
3 beaten eggs
1/4 cup cooked, crumbled bacon
1/2 cup blanched or steamed spinach (remove liquid before adding to omelet or cover and cook in microwave until wilted)
1-2 ounces of real Swiss cheese (1/4 - 1/2 cup)
Salt and pepper to taste
1-2 dollops of sour cream

### Instructions

Heat a 7-10 inch egg pan over

moderate heat. While the pan is heating, beat the eggs in a mixing bowl with a wire whip until blended but not frothy. When the pan is hot enough to sizzle a drop of water, add the butter and oil When the butter stops foaming, whip the eggs a couple of times and pour into the pan.

Let the eggs sit until they begin to cook around the edges. Lift the edges of the eggs with a rubber spatula and tip the pan to allow the liquid to run underneath. Repeat this process until the top is thickening and very little liquid egg remains.

Add the bacon, Swiss cheese and blanched spinach across the bottom of the omelet and add salt and pepper, if desired. Fold in half and slide onto plate. If serving two, cut in half before sliding onto plates. Garnish with a dollop of sour cream.

## Baked Swiss Steak

### *Ingredients*

2 lb round steak
1/3 cup flour
1/4 cup oil or shortening
1 1/2 teaspoons salt optional
1/8 teaspoon pepper
2 onions thinly sliced
1 can whole tomatoes
1 tablespoon Worcestershire sauce

### *Instructions*

Trim fat from steak and cut into serving pieces. Pound flour into both sides of steak. Heat fat in skillet; brown steak on both sides, season with salt and pepper. Place in Pyrex dish; cover with onion slices. In the same skillet, heat tomatoes, loosening brown bits from the bottom of the skillet. Add Worcestershire sauce and season to taste with salt and pepper. Pour over steak, cover with lid or foil and bake at 350°F for 2-2 1/2 hours, till fork tender. Serve over rice, buttered noodles or mashed potatoes.

**Creole Swiss Steak**

## *Ingredients*

1 1/2 pounds round steak
Seasoned flour
4 tablespoons butter or margarine
3/4 cup thinly sliced bell pepper
3/4 cup onion, sliced into rings
1 cup sliced mushrooms
1 cup hot water
3/4 cup tomato juice
1 bay leaf
1/8 teaspoon thyme
1/8 teaspoon sage
1/8 teaspoon nutmeg

## *Instructions*

Roll meat in flour. Sauté in skillet with 2 tablespoons of the butter. Place in baking dish. Melt remaining butter in skillet and sauté the bell pepper, onion and mushrooms until onions are clear. Add remaining ingredients, blending well. Spread over meat in baking dish. Cover and bake for 1 3/4 hours.

This can also be cooked on top of the stove by covering tightly and cooking on low for 1 1/2 hours. Serve over rice or mashed potatoes.

Serves 4 to 6.

## Crockpot Swiss Steak

### *Ingredients*

6 cube steaks
2 cans cream of mushroom soup
1 packet onion soup mix
1/2 cup water

### *Instructions*

Place all the ingredients in a crock pot. Simmer on low heat all day. Garnish with rice or mashed potatoes and serve.


## Swiss Cheese and Crab Pie

### *Ingredients*

1 cup Swiss cheese (or cheddar), shredded
8 oz crab meat
3 beaten eggs
3/4 cup heavy cream
1/4 cup water
1/2 teaspoon salt
dry mustard to taste

### *Instructions*

Heat the oven to 325°F. Sprinkle the cheese in a pie pan, lightly sprayed with PAM. Top with crab. Mix the remaining ingredients and pour over the top. Bake for 40-45 min.


## Mushroom and Swiss Patty      Melt With Peas

## Ingredients

1/4 pound ground turkey, formed into a patty
salt and ground pepper to taste
2 teaspoons extra virgin olive oil
1/2 small onion, sliced
1/2 cup sliced mushrooms
1/4 cup frozen peas
2 tablespoons grated Swiss cheese

## Instructions

Season patty with salt and pepper. Heat oil in a large skillet over medium-high heat; cook patty until golden brown on one side, about 3-4 minutes. Flip patty and move to one side of the skillet. Add onions, mushrooms, salt and pepper to the vacant side of the skillet; cook until softened and golden brown, about 5 minutes. Add peas and cook for one minute longer.
Sprinkle patty with cheese and transfer to a plate. Spoon hot vegetable mix over patty and serve.

Source: "Foodista.com – The Cooking Encyclopedia Everyone Can Edit".


**Mushroom-Swiss Hamburger Pie**

## Ingredients

2 teaspoons olive oil, divded
1 medium sweet onion, diced
12 ounces bottle of stout beer (I used Dark Horse Brewing Company'
1 teaspoon dried thyme
1 tablespoon Dijon mustard
teaspoon salt and fresh ground

pepper to taste
1 1/2 pounds lean ground beef (93 percent lean or better)
1 cup fresh whole wheat bread crumbs (I used a food processor to turn 3 pieces of high-fiber 1/4 cup parsley, chopped
1 large egg and 1 egg white, lightly beaten
10 ounces baby bella mushrooms, thickly sliced
3 ounces low-fat Swiss cheese, shredded

## *Instructions*

1. Preheat oven to 375°F (190°C)
2. Heat 1 teaspoon oil in a large skillet over medium heat and saute onions until translucent and just turning brown. Open the beer, take a sip and pour the rest in with the onions. Increase heat to medium-high and cook down until thick and syrupy.
3. Pour onion mixture into a large bowl, stir in thyme, mustard, salt and pepper and let cool. Add ground beef, breadcrumbs, parsley and eggs and mix thoroughly with clean hands.
4. Spray 9-inch pie plate with non stick and spread hamburger mixture evenly across the bottom and up the sides. Bake until meat reaches a temperature of 160F. Remove from oven and let stand 5 minutes.
5. Meanwhile, heat remaining oil over medium heat and lightly saute mushrooms.
6. Drain any fat from meat and top with mushrooms and shredded cheese. Turn oven to broil and cook until cheese is melted.
7. Makes 6 servings.

Source: "Foodista.com – The Cooking Encyclopedia Everyone Can Edit".


**Onion Swiss Steak**

## Ingredients

3 lb round steak, cut into 3/4 inch strips
1 1/2 teaspoon salt
1/4 teaspoon pepper
2 pkg dry onion soup mix
2 cloves garlic, minced
1 large can tomatoes
1 teaspoon oregano

## Instructions

Salt and pepper steak and place into oven. Sprinkle onion soup mix over top. Add garlic, oregano, and tomatoes. Cover and cook on low fire for 2-3 hours until meat is tender.


**Pressure Cooker Swiss Pepper Steak**

## Ingredients

2 lbs round steak - cut into serving size pieces
1 tablespoon olive oil - or more if needed
1 can beef broth - (14.5oz)
1 tablespoon dehydrated onion flakes
1/2 teaspoon salt and pepper
1 teaspoon garlic powder
1 teaspoon onion powder
3/4 cup sliced onion
2 medium green bell peppers - cut into chunks

## Instructions

Salt and pepper the steak and brown in oil in the pressure cooker. Add remaining ingredients and close cooker, bringing pressure up to full, then reduce heat and cook under full pressure for 15 minutes. Turn off heat and let cooker sit for 15 minutes, then release remaining pressure and serve.

## Rösti With Papaya Salad

### *Ingredients*

4 medium size potatoes, peeled and grated
1 onion medium size, finely chopped
1/4 cup bread crumbs (more or less)
2 inches piece- ginger, grated
1/4 teaspoon pepper powder (more or less)
salt to taste
olive oil to pan fry

For the Papaya Salad
2 cups raw papaya, peeled and grated
2 green chilli, slit through the middle, seeds removed
1/2 of a medium size red chilli, cut into rounds
1 teaspoon sunflower oil
1/4 teaspoon mustard seeds
1/4 teaspoon turmeric powder (haldi)
salt to taste

### *Instructions*

1. Heat oil in a pan, add the mustard seeds, when they begin to splutter, add the chillies and turmeric powder. Add the grated papaya and salt and cook for a couple of minutes and keep it aside.
2. Squeeze out the excess water from the grated potatoes.
3. Place the grated potatoes, onions, bread crumbs, ginger, pepper powder and salt in a bowl and mix well.
4. Take a little portion of the potato mixture, make a ball and gently

flatten it.

5.Sprinkle a few drops of oil on a non stick pan and pan fry the rösti on a low flame till both the sides are evenly golden.

6.Place the rosti on a serving dish, top it with the papya salad, garnish it with the chillies and serve.

Yield: 6 röstis

Source: "Foodista.com – The Cooking Encyclopedia Everyone Can Edit".

**Rösti**

## *Ingredients*

2 pounds red potatoes
1 1/2 cup onions
1/4-1/2 cup bacon, chopped into small pieces
1 teaspoon each salt and pepper (or to taste)
1 teaspoon cornstarch
2 tablespoons bacon fat or butter
2 tablespoons olive oil

## *Instructions*

Grate potatoes into long thin strips. Rinse in cold water. Squeeze dry in a dish towel to remove moisture. In a bowl mix potatoes and cornstarch. Add onions and bacon, and season with salt and pepper and mix. In a large skillet heat 2/3 of the fat/oil to medium heat. Add the potato mixture. Cook covered for 5-6 minutes, then uncovered for 3-4 minutes more until the bottom is golden. Flip over and cook the other side. Add the remaining fat/oil as necessary to prevent sticking.

Source: "Foodista.com – The Cooking Encyclopedia Everyone Can Edit".

## Raclette with Shrimps

### *Ingredients*

400 g Raclette cheese
100 g shrimps
75 g asparagus
500 g potatoes

### *Instructions*

Wash and boil potatoes in salted water with their skins on until tender. Keep in a warm place.

Put in the frying pan cheese and shrimps and melt the cheese for 5-6 minutes.

Peel and slice thin potatoes. Put on a serving plate. Top with asparagus. And pour with melted cheese with shrimps.

Serves 2.

## Rostis With Smoked Salmon and Dill Creme

### *Ingredients*

200 grams potatoes
2 eggs, beaten
30 grams butter, melted
125 ml crème fraiche
1 small bunch fresh dill, chopped

2 teaspoons lemon juice
100 grams smoked salmon, sliced

## *Instructions*

1. Preheat the oven to 200°C. Grate the potatoes into a colander and squeeze out excess moisture with your hands.
2. In a bowl, combine the potato and egg and season to taste. Lightly grease 12 mini muffin trays and fill with spoonfuls of the potato mixture.
3. Pour some butter over each rosti and bake for 20 minutes or until golden.
4. For the dill cream, combine the crème fraiche, dill and lemon juice.
5. To serve, arrange the salmon slices on top of the rostis. Top with dill cream, garnish with sprigs of dill and slivers of lemon.

Source: "Foodista.com – The Cooking Encyclopedia Everyone Can Edit".


**Savory Swiss Steak**

## *Ingredients*

3 3/4 pounds Beef, bottom round steaks
1 1/4 ounces All-purpose flour
1 1/2 teaspoons Salt
1/2 teaspoon Black pepper - ground
3 ounces Vegetable oil
10 ounces Onion - small dice
3 ounces Celery - small dice
2 teaspoons Garlic cloves - minced
2 ounces Tomato purée
1 1/2 ounces All-purpose flour

20 fluid ounces Beef stock
2 fluid ounces Soy Sauce


Sachet d'epices
4 Parsley stems - chopped
1 Cloves - whole
1 Bay leaf
2 Thyme sprig
2 Tarragon stem

## *Instructions*

Salt and pepper the steaks. Dredge the steaks with flour removing any excess. Flatten the steaks, then dredge them with flour again.

Preheat the oil in a large sauté pan. Place the steaks in the pan and brown them on both sides. Remove them to a braising pan.

Add the onions, celery, and garlic to the pan in which you browned the steaks, and stirring frequently sauté over medium heat until the vegetables become lightly browned and tender (6-8 minutes).

Add the tomato purée and continue to cook over medium heat until sweet and lightly browned (2 minutes). Add the flour and stir for 3-4 minutes until the mixture is evenly blended and pasty. Add the stock and soy sauce and stir or whisk until very smooth. Bring this braising liquid to a simmer and cook constantly stirring 3-4 minutes. Pour the liquid over the steaks in the braising pan and cover tightly. Place the braising pan in the oven at a temperature of 350°F and braise 40-45 minutes until the steaks become almost tender. Remove the cover and continue cooking periodically turning the steaks to get them evenly coated with the braising liquid.

Combine the thyme, tarragon, parsley, bay leaf, and cloves in a piece of cheesecloth to make a sachet. Put the sachet in the braising liquid and continue to braise 30-35 minutes more until the steaks are fork-tender.

Transfer the steaks to a holding pan. Moisten them with a little of the braising liquid, cover, and keep warm.

Pour the braising liquid (without sachet) into a saucepan. Bring to a simmer over medium-high heat. Skim off any grease or oil from the liquid surface. Let the liquid simmer until it is slightly reduced and has a good flavor (about 10 minutes). Strain the liquid and salt and pepper to taste. Serve the steak with 2 fluid ounces of the hot sauce on heated plates.

Serves 10.

**Spam Swiss Pie**

## Ingredients

1 9-inch deep dish pie shell
6 eggs
1 cup whipping cream
1/8 teaspoon pepper
1 12-oz can Spam luncheon meat - cubed
1/4 cup chopped onion
2 cups shredded Swiss cheese -- divided

## Instructions

Preheat the oven to 425°F. Bake the pie shell for 6-8 minutes. Reduce the temperature to 350°F.

Combine in the bowl eggs, whipping cream, and pepper. Beat the mixture. Stir in spam and onions. Sprinkle 1 cup cheese in the pie shell. Pour egg mixture over the cheese. Sprinkle remaining cheese over egg.

Bake 45-55 minutes or until the eggs are set.

## Speedy Swiss Steak

### *Ingredients*

1 1/2 lb round steak (1/2 inch thick)
3/4 teaspoon meat tenderizer, unseasoned
1 tablespoon oil
2 tablespoons flour
1 teaspoon onion powder
1/8 teaspoon garlic powder
15 oz tomato sauce
1 celery stalk, chopped
1 teaspoon sugar

### *Instructions*

Cut meat into serving sized pieces. Moisten meat, lightly, with water. Sprinkle meat with tenderizer on each side of the steak. Allow to stand 10 to 15 minutes. Heat oil in a large skillet. Sprinkle meat with flour. Add meat to hot oil and brown 2 to 3 minutes. Turn meat and add onion. Cook 2 to 3 minutes more or until meat is well browned. Add all remaining ingredients and reduce heat. Cover and simmer 30 minutes or until meat is tender.

## Swiss Bacon and Eggs

### *Ingredients*

8 large eggs 1/4 cup milk 1/2 teaspoon salt 1/4 teaspoon pepper 1/3 cups finely chopped green onion 4 oz Swiss cheese cooking spray

## Instructions

Preheat the broiler. In a medium mixing bowl, whisk together eggs, milk, salt and pepper until well blended. Stir in all ingredients except for 2 tablespoons onions.

Place 12" skillet over mid-low heat until hot. Coat the skillet with a cooking spray. Add egg mixture. Cover tightly and cook for 14 min or until almost set. Arrange bacon in pinwheel on top of the egg mixture. Top with cheese and place under broiler for 2 minutes or until the cheese is bubbly. Top with the remaining 2 tablespoons onion. Cut into 4 wedges and serve immediately.

**Swiss Chalet Dip**

## Ingredients

1 cup dry white wine
2 cups Swiss cheese shredded
1 tablespoon unbleached flour
1 tablespoon brandy
1 garlic clove crushed in press
1 tablespoon white onion finely diced
black pepper to taste 1/4
c smoked ham finely diced

## Instructions

Place the wine in a saucepan over medium-high heat. Mix the Swiss cheese and flour together and gradually add to the wine, stirring constantly, until all the cheese is melted and mixture is smooth. Remove from the heat and add the brandy, garlic, onion, pepper, and ham. Pour into a chafing dish and sprinkle with nutmeg. Serve hot.

Makes about 3 1/4 cups of dip.

SUGGESTED DIPPERS: Apples, Artichoke Hearts, Crackers, French Bread Chunks, Ham, Salami

**Swiss Chard With Cheese**

## *Ingredients*

2 lb. swiss chard
2 tablespoons butter or margarine
2 tablespoons. flour
1 teaspoon salt
1/2 cup milk
1/2 lb. diced pasteurized process cheese
1/2 cup bread crumbs
2 tablespoons melted butter

## *Instructions*

Cut stalks from washed chard leaves in 1 inch pieces. Place in bottom of large kettle, cover with boiling water (salted). Cover and cook 5 minutes. Add torn leaves and continue cooking for 5 more minutes. Drain in colander, pressing out liquid. (5 cups chard) Melt butter, blend in flour and salt. Add milk and cook over low heat, stirring constantly until mixture thickens. Add cheese, stirring until cheese is melted and blended. Place chard into greased dish. Pour cheese over top and sprinkle with crumbs that have been coated with butter.

Swiss Chard With Cheese

**Swiss Cheddar Fondue**

## Ingredients

3 cloves of Garlic, Minced
5 1/2 cups of White Wine
1 teaspoon of Lemon Juice
8 ounces of Shredded White Cheddar
8 ounces of Shredded Emmentaler Swiss
3 tablespoons of Corn Starch
1 tablespoon of Brandy or Kirsch
1/2 teaspoon of Nutmeg
Salt to Taste

## Instructions

1. Start out by rubbing the minced garlic around the inside of your pot (or the pot your cooking it in if you're planning to transfer the cheese after cooking on the stove). If you love garlic like I do, then you can just leave it there and let it meld with the cheese. If not, then simply remove the bits.
2. Next up, you'll add in the wine and allow it to warm up to a simmer.
3. In a bowl, mix together the two cheeses along with the corn starch.
4. When the wine is heated up, add in your cheese, one handful at a time. Let each handful melt completely; stirring to combine well before adding the next.
5. Once all of your cheese is melted and smooth, add in the nutmeg and brandy.
6. Transfer to a fondue pot if you haven't already and prepare to dip, swirl, and dunk your way to culinary bliss.

Source: "Foodista.com – The Cooking Encyclopedia Everyone Can Edit".

## Swiss Cheese and Sausage Deep Dish

### *Ingredients*

8 ounces Brown & Serve sausages
1 cup Bisquick® baking mix
1/4 cup cold water
6 ounces shredded Swiss cheese
2 eggs
1/4 cup milk
1/4 teaspoon salt
1/8 teaspoon pepper

### *Instructions*

Cook the sausages as directed on the package. Drain. Preheat the oven to 375 °F. Grease a round pan, 9 x 1-1/2-inch. Mix the baking mix and water until soft dough is formed. Beat strongly 20 strokes. Press the dough at the bottom and 1 inch up side of the pan with fingers floured with baking mix. Place the sausages in a spoke pattern on the dough. Sprinkle with cheese. Beat the eggs with a fork; stir in milk. Add salt and pepper. Stir. Pour over the sausages and cheese. Bake for about 25 minutes until puffed and golden brown.


## Swiss Cheese Chicken Casserole

### *Ingredients*

4-6 chicken breasts
6 slices Swiss cheese
1 can cream of mushroom soup
1/4 cup milk
2 cups Pepperidge Farm herb seasoning stuffing mix

1/4 cup margarine

## Instructions

Place chicken in casserole lightly greased. Place cheese on top of chicken. Mix soup and milk and pour over chicken. Cover mixture up with stuffing mix. Drizzle butter over crumbs. Cover and bake at 350°F for 50 minutes.

**Swiss Cheese Fondue**

## Ingredients

2 cup White wine (good stuff, not from the grocery store)
1 clove Garlic
1 lb. Swiss cheese
3 tablespoons Corn starch or flour
1 teaspoon Salt
1-2 tablespoons Worcestershire sauce
1/4 teaspoon Pepper

## Instructions

1. Heat 1 3/4 cups wine and garlic clove until just before it boils - don't boil
2. Remove garlic clove, turn down heat, add cheese stirring constantly, until melted. (Add a little at a time)
3. Combine cornstarch, salt, Worcestershire sauce, pepper, with 1/4 cup cheese. Stir until smooth. Dip pieces of French bread into fondue with forks.

Source: http://fresh-recipes.wikidot.com/swiss-cheese-fondue.

## Swiss Cheese Meat Loaf

### *Ingredients*

1 lb. of Ground beef
8 slices of Swiss cheese
1/4 cup of chopped onion
1/2 cup of dry breadcrumbs
1 egg
2 cans of tomato sauce
3/4 cup milk
1 teaspoon salt
1/4 teaspoon pepper
1/4 teaspoon thyme

### *Instructions*

Mix all the ingredients in a bowl except for cheese. Put half of the mixture in a greased loaf pan. Put the cheese on top of the meat mixture. Then put the rest of the meat mixture on top of the cheese. Bake at 350°F for 1 to 1 1/2 hours.


## Swiss Chicken

### *Ingredients*

1 stick margarine or butter
1/2 cup milk
10 chicken breast halves, deboned
10 slices Swiss cheese
1 can cream of chicken soup
1 pkg. Pepperidge Farm herb dressing mix

### *Instructions*

Place chicken breast in large flat baking dish. Sprinkle with salt and pepper (salt sparingly). Place 1 slice of cheese on top of each breast. Mix can of soup with 1/2 cup milk and pour over chicken. Melt margarine or butter and mix with dressing mix and spread over chicken. Bake at 325°F degrees uncovered for 1 1/2 hours.

Swiss Chicken

**Swiss Fried Potatoes (Rösti)**

## Ingredients

4 medium potatoes
1/4 cup butter or margarine
1 small onion, chopped
1/2 cup diced Gruyère or Swiss cheese
1/2 teaspoon salt
1/4 teaspoon pepper
2 tablespoons water

## Instructions

Heat 1 inch salted water to boiling. Add potatoes. Heat to boiling; reduce heat. Cover and cook until tender, 30 to 35 minutes. Peel and shred potatoes or cut into 1/4-inch strips. Heat butter in skillet until melted. Add potatoes, onion and cheese. Sprinkle with salt and pepper. Cook uncovered over medium heat, turning frequently, until potatoes start to brown, about 10 minutes, adding 1 to 2 tablespoons butter to prevent sticking if necessary.

Press potatoes with spatula to form a flat cake; sprinkle with water. Cover and cook over low heat, without stirring, until bottom is golden brown and crusty, about 10 minutes. Place inverted platter over skillet; invert potatoes onto platter.

Yields 4 to 6 servings.

## Swiss Omelet Roll

### *Ingredients*

1 1/2 cup mayonnaise, divided
2 tablespoons mustard
1/2 cup chopped scallions, divided
2 tablespoons flour
1 cup milk
12 eggs, separated
1/2 teaspoon salt
1/8 teaspoon pepper
Cooking spray
1 1/2 cup finely chopped ham
1 cup shredded Swiss cheese
Watercress to garnish (optional)

### *Instructions*

Combine 1 cup mayonnaise, mustard and 1/4 cup scallions. Mix well and set aside. Combine remaining mayonnaise and flour. Gradually add milk and beaten egg yolks. Cook, stirring constantly over low heat, until thickened. Remove from heat and cool 15 minutes. Beat egg whites until stiff. Fold mayonnaise mixture, salt and pepper into whites, combining thoroughly. Pour into a 15 x 10-inch jellyroll pan lined with wax paper coated with cooking spray. Bake at 425°F for 20 minutes.

Invert on towel. Carefully remove the wax paper. Mix the ham, cheese and 1/4 cup scallions together and spread on the roll. Roll from narrow end, lifting with towel while rolling. Place on serving dish seam down and top with the mustard sauce.

Garnish with the greenery of your choice. Watercress is especially nice.

Serves 6-8.

## Swiss Parmesan Potato Casserole

### *Ingredients*

1 1/4 cups grated parmesan cheese
1/2 teaspoon salt
1/8 teaspoon pepper
6 potatoes, peeled and thinly sliced
6 tablespoons butter
1/2 cup cream
1/2 cup grated Swiss cheese
2 tablespoons chopped chives

### *Instructions*

Heat the oven to 400°F. Mix parmesan, salt and pepper. Butter 2-quart casserole dish.

Layer potatoes in a dish, sprinkling each layer with the cheese mixture. Grease with butter and cover tightly with foil. Bake for one hour.

Uncover and pour cream over the top. Sprinkle with Swiss cheese. Bake uncovered for 5 minutes until the cheese melts. Sprinkle with chives before serving.

## Swiss Roll Rice

### *Ingredients*

Part I - for Fish Paste Roll
150 g Fish Paste

1 Egg, beaten
2 drops of Oil

Part II - for Sushi or my Swiss Roll
Rice
Furikake (dry Japanese condiment)

## *Instructions*

Part I
1. Heat pan with oil.
2. Pour half of the beaten egg into the pan.
3. Swirl the pan to let the egg spread out.
4. Remove egg when it's cooked.
5. Repeat with the remaining half of the beaten egg. Spread fish paste thinly over one egg crepe.
6. Place the second egg crepe on top of the fish paste.
7. Spread fish paste thinly it.
8. Start rolling it (like sushi).
9. Tuck in the ends.
10. Place on a plate and cover with cling wrap (to avoid water from getting it and making the egg soggy)
11. Steam for 10 minutes or till cooked.
12. Remove, sliced into smaller pieces and serve.

Part II
1. Place rice on clingwrap covered bamboo mat.
2. Place above fish paste roll on one end of the rice.
3. Roll like how you would do for a sushi.
4. Cut it in portion.
5. Top with some Furikake and serve.

Source: "Open Source Food" - opensourcefood.com.

## Swiss Scrambled Eggs

### *Ingredients*

4 tablespoons margarine
2 tablespoon onion flakes
1/2 cups water
4 tablespoon dry milk
1 cup shredded Swiss cheese
2 teaspoons Worcestershire sauce
12 eggs, beaten
salt and pepper to taste
Tobasco to taste

### *Instructions*

Melt margarine in large skillet. Add onion flakes. Combine water, dry milk, Worcestershire sauce, and cheese, and add to eggs. Pour the mixture into skillet and cook on low heat, stirring until set. Season to taste with Tobasco, salt and pepper.

## Swiss Sour Cream Casserole

### *Ingredients*

2 teaspoons olive or vegetable oil
1 cup diced onions
1 cup sliced mushroom caps
2 teaspoons all-purpose flour
1 1/2 cups water
2 envelopes instant beef broth and seasoning mix

1 tablespoon grated Parmesan cheese
1 teaspoon Worcestershire sauce
1/4 teaspoon paprika
Dash of pepper
4 (5 ounce) beef top or bottom round steaks, broiled until rare
1/2 cup sour cream
1 tablespoon chopped fresh parsley

## *Instructions*

Preheat the oven to 350°F. Prepare oil in a skillet. Add onions and mushrooms. Sauté, stirring, until the onions become almost transparent. Sprinkle vegetables with flour. Cook, stirring constantly, for 1 minute. Stir in water gradually.

Add broth mix and bring it to boil. Reduce heat and let it simmer until the mixture thickens. Stir in cheese. Stir in Worcestershire sauce. Stir in paprika and pepper. Remove from heat.

Transfer steaks to another casserole and pour vegetable sauce over meat. Cover and bake until the steaks are tender for about 45 minutes. Remove the steaks from casserole and set aside.

Combine 2 tablespoons of vegetable sauce and sour cream and stir. Pour the sour cream mixture into the casserole and stir well. Return the steaks to the casserole and serve sprinkled with parsley.

Serves 4.

Source: "Foodista.com – The Cooking Encyclopedia Everyone Can Edit".

**Swiss Vegetable Medley**

## *Ingredients*

1 bag (16 oz.) frozen broccoli, carrots, cauliflower combination (thawed and drained)
1 can (10 3/4 oz.) condensed cream of mushroom soup
1 cup (4 oz.) shredded swiss cheese
1/3 cup sour cream
1/4 teaspoon pepper
1 can Durkee french fried onions

## *Instructions*

Combine vegetables, soup, 1/2 cup cheese, sour cream, pepper and 1/2 can onions. Pour into quart casserole. Bake covered at 350°F for 30 minutes. Top with remaining cheese and onions. Bake uncovered 5 minutes longer.

Makes 6 servings.


**Traditional Swiss Raclette**

## *Ingredients*

250 grams per persons Raclette cheese sliced
2 per persons Small potatoes, called New Potatoes or fingerlings and a variety of other names
200 grams per persons Bundnerfleisch, sliced air-dried beef
1 jar Corninchons, dill baby gherkins
1 jar Cocktail Onions, drained
Paprika
Freshly Milled Black Pepper

## *Instructions*

1. About a half hour before grilling at the table, take the cheese out of the refrigerator, slice and set on a serving plate.
2. Wash and boil your baby potatoes in salted water with their skins

on until tender. Drain the water away and place potatoes on the dining table with the cheese and other accoutrements.

3. Arrange Bundnerfleisch slices decoratively on a serving plate. Find this at your favorite delicatessen. You can also substitute other meats.

4. Drain cornichons and cocktail onions and place either together or separate in bowls.

5. When ready to start eating, turn your raclette grill on and when hot begin heating the meats on top and the cheeses on the bottom level in the small cheese pans.

6. Meanwhile, place a potato on your own plate with some cornichons and onions and when the meat is heated and the cheese melted, add those to your plate as well.

7. Dust with freshly ground black pepper and paprika.

Source: "Foodista.com – The Cooking Encyclopedia Everyone Can Edit".

**Traditional Swiss Raclette**

*Ingredients*

250 grams per persons Raclette cheese sliced
2 per persons Small potatoes, called New Potatoes or fingerlings and a variety of other names
200 grams per persons Bundnerfleisch, sliced air-dried beef
1 jar Corninchons, dill baby gherkins
1 jar Cocktail Onions, drained
Paprika
Freshly Milled Black Pepper

*Instructions*

1. About a half hour before grilling at the table, take the cheese out

of the refrigerator, slice and set on a serving plate.
2. Wash and boil your baby potatoes in salted water with their skins on until tender. Drain the water away and place potatoes on the dining table with the cheese and other accoutrements.
3. Arrange Bundnerfleisch slices decoratively on a serving plate. Find this at your favorite delicatessen. You can also substitute other meats.
4. Drain cornichons and cocktail onions and place either together or separate in bowls.
5. When ready to start eating, turn your raclette grill on and when hot begin heating the meats on top and the cheeses on the bottom level in the small cheese pans.
6. Meanwhile, place a potato on your own plate with some cornichons and onions and when the meat is heated and the cheese melted, add those to your plate as well.
7. Dust with freshly ground black pepper and paprika.

Source: "Foodista.com – The Cooking Encyclopedia Everyone Can Edit".

**Vegan Swiss Fondue**

## *Ingredients*

3 cups water
1/4 cups fresh lemon juice
1/4 cups tahini
1/2 teaspoon mustard powder
4 teaspoons onion granules
1/2 cup nutritional yeast flakes
1/3 cup quick cooking rolled oats
4 tablespoons arrowroot powder
1 teaspoon salt

## Instructions

Place all ingredients into a blender and process until very smooth. Pour into a saucepan and bring to a boil, stirring constantly. Reduce the heat to low, and continue to cook for a few more minutes, stirring constantly, until thick and smooth. Transfer to a fondue pot, and keep warm over a very low flame.

Source: http://vegetarian-recipes.wikispaces.com/Vegan+Swiss+Fondue /

## Venison Swiss Steak #1

### Ingredients

1 1/2 - 2 lbs. venison steak
1 pkg. dry onion soup mix, water
flour
salt and pepper to taste
Shortening

### Instructions

Dredge meat in flour. Melt shortening, brown meat on both sides. Sprinkle with soup mix. Cover with water. Cover tightly. Simmer 1 1/2 hours or until done on top of stove or bake at 350°F until tender. Make gravy from remaining liquid and onion.

## Venison Swiss Steak #2

### Ingredients

2 venison steaks
1 cn cream of mushroom soup

2 sliced onions

## *Instructions*

Salt and pepper. Add several drops of worcestershire. Cut steaks into serving portions. Place in electric frying pan and add water to simmer meat, approximately 10 minutes on each side. Add remaining ingredients and more water, if necessary during cooking time. Cook on low heat 175 - 200 degrees F until tender (about one hour). Turn meat to prevent sticking. This can be adapted for stove top, slow cooker or oven cooking.

## Desserts, Baking and Beverages

**Baseler Leckerli (Swiss Spice Cookies)**

## *Ingredients*

4 1/2 cups flour
1 tablespoon cinnamon
1 1/2 teaspoons ground cloves
1 teaspoon ground cardamom
1/2 teaspoon nutmeg
1 teaspoon baking soda
1 cup honey
1/2 cup granulated sugar
2 tablespoons water
1/2 cup slivered unblanched almonds
1/2 cup candied orange peel, chopped
Grated zest of 1/2 lemon
Simple glaze

## *Instructions*

Preheat the oven to 350 degrees F. Line 2 baking sheets with parchment or liberally grease them.

Sift together the flour, cinnamon, cloves, cardamom, nutmeg and baking soda.

Combine the honey, sugar and water in a small saucepan. Place over low heat until the honey just melts. Do not let boil. (Or, combine the honey, sugar and water in a microwave-safe, large bowl, and microwave on medium for 1 minute, until the honey just melts.)

Transfer the mixture to the bowl of a heavy-duty mixer fitted with the dough hook. Let cool slightly.

Add the sifted flour mixture, the almonds, orange peel and lemon zest. Blend until the mixture comes together in a heavy, sticky dough, adding a spoonful or two of water if needed. (The mixing can be done by hand, but it's labor intensive.) Resist the urge to add more water to make the dough easier to handle; it would impair the texture of the finished cookies.

Spread the dough about 1/2 to 1 inch thick on the baking sheets, forming 3 rectangles, each about 8 x 9 inches.

Bake for about 20 minutes, until the tops turn a medium brown.

While the leckerli are baking, make the simple glaze.

When the dough rectangles have baked, remove pans to a rack and immediately brush the tops with glaze. Let cool for 10 minutes.

Cut into 1 x 3-inch bars or into diamond shapes. Transfer to racks to cool completely.

Store in airtight containers, placing wax paper between layers. Let age at least 1 week, preferably longer. No need to freeze these cookies - properly stored, they keep well throughout the holidays.

Yields 5 to 6 dozen cookies.

**Broccoli Onion Swiss Quiche**

## *Ingredients*

3 cups chopped broccoli - cooked, drained, cooled
1/2 cup chopped onion - favorite color
3 tablespoons butter -(or less)
1 1/2 tablespoons soy flour
3/4 teaspoon salt
pinch pepper and nutmeg to taste
3 eggs
1/2 cup heavy cream
with enough water to equal 2/3 cup liquid
4 slices cooked bacon - crumbled or cut in small pieces
2 ounces shredded swiss cheese

## *Instructions*

Prepare 9" pie plate sprayed with non-stick spray. Preheat to 375°F.

Set aside cooked broccoli.

Saute onions gently in butter, when tender add soy flour and cook a couple more minutes.

Whisk together eggs, cream and water. Blend in salt and spices.

Combine egg mix, prepared vegetables and cheese.

Pour into prepared pie plate.

Bake at temperature 375°F about 25 minutes until puffed and browned.

## Cheese Pie (Käse Wake)

### *Ingredients*

1 (9-inch) unbaked piecrust
1/2 pound Swiss cheese, grated
1 tablespoon flour
3 eggs, well beaten
1 cup milk
Salt and pepper, to taste

### *Instructions*

Combine cheese and flour. Spread in piecrust. Combine milk and eggs. Add salt and pepper and pour over cheese. Bake at 400 degrees F for 15 minutes. Reduce heat to 325 degrees F and bake 30 more minutes or until a knife inserted in center comes out clean.

Serves 6.

## Chocolate Fondue

### *Ingredients*

1 cup premium cocoa powder (example:Scharffen Berger), sifted
1 1/4 cup water
1 1/2 cups sugar
1/4 cup corn syrup
1/2 cup plus 5 tablespoon heavy cream
5 oz 62% Scharffen Berger (premium semi-sweet chocolate), chopped
Pound cake and fruit (example bananas, apples, strawberries,

plums), cut into bite sized pieces

## *Instructions*

First, sift the cocoa into mixing bowl and set aside. It helps create the smooth creamy texture that you want for serving.

Then, place the water, sugar, and corn syrup into a pot and bring to boil. Allow the mixture to simmer for 10-15 minutes until sugar solution has reduced by about 30%. Pour the cocoa powder a little bit at a time into the solution and blend with a whisk until nice and smooth.

Next, return the chocolate mixture to the stove and continue cooking over medium heat. Add the heavy cream, bring it to a boil and allow to simmer for five minutes. Remove from the heat and stir in your chopped chocolate. Pour it all into a ceramic fondue pot or one appropriate and keep warm until ready to serve.

To dip cut up pieces of cake and fruits.


**Christmas Swiss Roll**

## *Ingredients*

125 g (4 oz) caster sugar
75 g (3 oz) flour
3 eggs
30 ml (2 tablespoons) cocoa powder
can of sweetened chestnut paste 440 g (15.5 oz)
icing sugar
decoration, holly sprigs
oil for greasing

## *Instructions*

Prepare a swissroll cake tin, about 13 x 9 inch, inserting greaseproof paper into the greased tin and then greasing the paper itself. Shake a small amount of caster sugar around the tin, then do the same with some flour, finally shaking out the extra.

Whisk the eggs and sugar in a bowl placed over steam from water at just at boiling point. Be careful not to over heat the mixture. It should be just thick enough to make strands as you lift the whisk out of the ingredients.

Take thr mixture away from the heat and continue whisking as it cools, (about 5 minutes). Blend in the cocoa powder and flour followed by hot water (1 tablespoon).

Take the tin from step one and pour in the mixture. Bake at 200°C (400°F) until the cake has come away from the sides of the tin a bit (about 10 minutes).

Remove the cake from the tin and place on greaseproof paper, previously coated then shaken with caster sugar. Trim the hard edges off the cake, then bake the rolled up cake (with paper inside) for an additional 20 minutes.

Melt the chocolate with water (1 tablespoon) in a bowl placed over water just at boiling point. Mix icing sugar into some softened butter and then add the melted chocolate.

Take the cold swiss roll, unroll it and add the chestnut paste, spreading over the complete surface. Remove the paper, roll up again and put on a plate.

Attach a slice of the roll to the side of the log with butter cream. Preferably a diagonal slice.

Complete the presentation by using a piping bag with star shaped nozzle to run lines of butter cream along the swiss roll log. Finally, sprinkle with icing sugar and decorate with sprigs of holly.

## Eierochrli (Swiss Carnival Cakes)

### *Ingredients*

8 small eggs
1/2 cup cream
Pinch of salt
3 teaspoons confectioners' sugar
1 ounce butter, melted
Sifted flour, as needed

### *Instructions*

Mix ingredients for 15 minutes, adding enough sifted flour to make a dough; let stand for 15 minutes.

Form into small apple-size balls; roll as thin as possible, then pull carefully by hand to tissue paper thinness. Fry in butter in small pan; sprinkle at once with fine sugar. These can be stored for weeks.

## Garlic Bread

### *Ingredients*

7 ounces French bread
1 3/4 ounces butter
4 garlic clove - mashed
1/4 ounce Gruyere cheese - grated
1 tablespoon parsley
salt and freshly ground pepper to taste

### *Instructions*

Cut bread into slices, toast in oven. Beat butter until creamy, chop parsley finely, blend butter with garlic, cheese (Gruyere) and parsley. Salt and pepper to taste. Spread bread with butter mixture, gratinee under broiler until golden brown. Serve with soup.

## Matcha and mandarin swiss roll

### *Ingredients*

Dough:
* 4 eggs, white and yolk separated
* 50 grams of sugar
* 3 tablespoons of wheat flour
* 2 tablespoons of corn flour
* 1 teaspoon of matcha powder
* 1/2 teaspoon of baking powder

Mandarin mousse:
* 350 grams of cream
* 400 grams of mandarins
* 1 package of orange jelly

### *Instructions*

1. Whisk whites till they turn into firm foam.
2. Add sugar bit by bit while continue whisking.
3. Add yolks, one at a time, keep whisking.
4. Sift flours and matcha, mix well.
5. Add flour mixture bit by bit to the foam, stiring gently.
6. Line baking tray with baking paper, pour over dough. Form rectangle about 0,5 cm thick.
7. Bake in preheated oven in 180 C degrees, about 10 minutes.
8. When sponge cake is baked, put it on the kitchen cloth and roll.

9. Meanwhile prepare jelly using half of water (250 ml of water for packege of jelly calling for 500 ml).
10. Peal mandarins, divide and put into jelly.
11. Whip cream and add 3/4 of it to jelly and mix well. Wait till jelly is almost set.
12. Unroll the sponge cake, arrange mousse and roll.
13. Serve garnished with remaining whipped cream.

Source: "Open Source Food" - opensourcefood.com.

**Mocha Fondue**

*Ingredients*

8 oz Semisweet Chocolate
1/2 cup Hot Espresso or Coffee
3 tablespoons Granulated Sugar
2 tablespoons Butter
1/2 teaspoon Vanilla Extract

*Instructions*

Chop chocolate into small pieces and set aside. Heat espresso and sugar in fondue pot on low heat. Slowly add chocolate and butter while stirring. Add Vanilla.

Optional: Add a splash of Irish Cream.

To Dip: Angel Food Cake, Apple Slices, Bananas, Strawberries, Pound Cake, Pretzels, Pineapple Chunks, Marshmallows

**Pear Bread**

## Ingredients

2 cups scalded milk
3 cups granulated sugar
4 teaspoons salt
1 cup fat
2 cups water
3 packages active dry yeast
1 cup lukewarm water
3 pounds raisins
2 pounds dried pears
2 pounds currants
1 to 2 tablespoons anise powder
2 teaspoons cinnamon
Flour

## Instructions

Combine scalded milk, sugar, salt, fat and water. Cool to lukewarm. Soften yeast in the lukewarm water. Stir in the yeast and enough flour to make a sponge dough. Add the fruit and enough flour to make a dough that will not stick to the board. Put into a bowl and let rise until double.

Shape into loaves and let rise again until double. Bake at 225°F about 2 hours.

**Swiss Almond Macaroons**

## Ingredients

1/3 cup whole blanched almonds
1/2 cup + 3 tablespoons sugar
1/2 teaspoon vanilla
1 tablespoon water
2 large egg whites
1/4 cup whipping cream
1/4 lb semisweet chocolate, finely cut

## *Instructions*

Process almonds and 3 tablespoons sugar in food processor bowl fitted with metal blade, pulsing on and off, until very finely ground. Add vanilla. Pulse again and scrape inside of work bowl with metal spatula. Add water and pulse again to mix. Leave almond mixture in work bowl while preparing meringue.

Whisk egg whites and 1/2 cup sugar in mixer bowl. Place bowl over pan of simmering water and whisk until egg whites are hot and sugar is dissolved, about 2 minutes. Whip meringue until cooled and fluffy. Add about 1/4 of meringue to work bowl containing almond mixture and pulse to mix. Add another 1/4 of meringue to work bowl and pulse to mix again. Remove blade and scrape almond meringue mixture from work bowl onto remaining whites. Fold into egg whites.

Scrape almond-meringue mixture into pastry. bag fitted with plain tube that has 1/4-inch opening. Cover two baking pans with parchment paper. Pipe 24 (1/2-inch) macaroons on each pan (48 total), leaving 1 inch between macaroons. Bake macaroons at 375 degrees until lightly golden, about 15 minutes. (Switch pans from back to front and top to bottom once or twice during baking. ) Cool macaroons on pans. When cool, remove from parchment paper.

Bring cream to boil in saucepan. Remove from heat. Add chocolate and allow to stand 2 minutes. Whisk smooth. Scrape filling into bowl to cool.

To assemble, place dab of chocolate filling on flat side of 24 baked macaroons. Press flat sides of remaining 24 macaroons against filling. Store in cool place. Serve macaroons on day they are prepared.

**Swiss Apple Pie**

## Ingredients

6 cups Peeled apples, cut in 1 inch wedges
2 teaspoons Lemon juice
1 tablespoon Flour
1/3 cup White sugar
1/4 cup Brown sugar
1/2 teaspoon Cinnamon
1/4 teaspoon Nutmeg
1/4 teaspoon Salt
1/8 teaspoon Ginger
1 tablespoon Butter

## Instructions

This scrumptious spicy apple pie is served with a hot brandy sauce. Pastry of your choice cream or milk hot brandy sauce. Sprinkle apple wedges with lemon juice and toss well. Combine remaining ingredients except butter, cream and sauce. Line a 9 inch pie plate with half the pastry and sprinkle bottom with 1/3 of the sugar spice mix. Top with half the apple wedges, fitting them in as tightly as possible. Sprinkle with another third of the sugar spice mix. Top with the rest of apples and sprinkle with remaining sugar spice mix. Press gently with your hand, to make it as compact as possible. Dot with butter, and top with remaining pastry. Brush top with cream or milk. Bake in a 425°F oven 15 minutes. Reduce heat to 350°F and bake 40-45 minutes, or until crust is golden brown.

**Swiss Cheese and Crab Pie**

## Ingredients

1 cup Swiss cheese (or cheddar), shredded
8 oz crab meat

3 beaten eggs
3/4 cup heavy cream
1/4 cup water
1/2 teaspoon salt
dry mustard to taste

## *Instructions*

Heat oven to 325°F. Sprinkle cheese in pie pan, lightly sprayed with PAM. Top with crab. Mix remaining ingredients and pour over top. Bake 40-45 min.

### Swiss Cheese Gougere

## *Ingredients*

1 cup Water
1/4 cup Butter or margarine
1 cup All purpose flour
1 teaspoon Oregano
4 Eggs
1/2 teaspoon Salt
1 cup Swiss cheese; shredded
pepper

## *Instructions*

In 2 qt saucepan, combine water, butter, oregano, salt and pepper. Bring to a roiling boil. Stir until butter is melted. Add flour, all at once. Stir to make a thick ball of dough that clings together. Beat in eggs, one at a time. Beat until dough is satiny smooth. Mix in cheese. Generously grease a baking sheet. Spoon 6 mounds of dough onto sheet in a ring formation, close enough so that they touch each other. Bake at 375°F for 55-60 minutes or until golden brown. Serve hot with sweet butter. For breakfast serve with jam or preserves.

## Swiss Cheese Potato Bread

### *Ingredients*

3 cups bread or all-purpose flour
1 package dry yeast
1 teaspoon sugar
1 teaspoon salt
1/4 cup instant potato flakes
1 1/2 cups hot water, 120-130°F
1/2 stick butter or margarine, melted
2 eggs
4 ounces Swiss cheese, coarsely grated

### *Instructions*

Put 1 1/2 cups flour into a large mixing bowl and stir in the yeast, sugar, salt, potato flakes, and hot water. Beat for 1 minute with the mixer. Add the melted butter or margarine, eggs, and Swiss cheese. Beat with mixer for 2 minutes.

Stir in the rest of the flour by portions of 1/2 cup at a time. Stir first with the spoon and then by hand, or with the mixer flat beater and then dough hook. The dough will be a rough, shaggy mass that will clean the sides of the bowl. However, if it still slack (wet), add small portions of flour.

Transfer the dough onto a floured work surface and knead it. Add light sprinkles of flour if necessary. Then put the dough in the mixer, with the dough hook. The dough will completely clean the sides of the bowl and form a ball around the revolving hook. The dough will be smooth and elastic. Knead it by hand or mixer for 8 minutes.

Place the dough in a greased mixing bowl and pat with buttered or greased fingers. Cover the bowl tightly with plastic wrap and leave to stand about 1 hour at room temperature until the dough has doubled in volume .

Punch down the dough, turn it onto the floured work surface, and let it rest for 2 minutes. It can be shaped in one of two ways. One is to roll it under your palms to about 20 inches in length. Lay the length of dough in the prepared pan. Overlap the ends slightly and pinch together. The second way is to flatten the ball of dough and with fingers punch a hole in the center and widen this to slip over the tube. Either way, push the dough firmly into the bottom of the pan.

Cover the pan with a length of foil or wax paper and let it rise for 45 minutes until the dough has doubled in volume.

Preheat the oven to 375°F 20 minutes before baking. Bake about 45 minutes until you insert a skewer in the loaf and it comes out clean and dry. Ten minutes before the end of baking, carefully transfer the loaf onto a baking sheet. And place the sheet back to the oven. This will give the loaf a lovely overall brown color. But handle it carefully. It is fragile when hot.

Take the bread from the oven. Slide the loaf onto a metal rack to cool before slicing.

**Swiss Chocolate Brownies**

*Ingredients*

1 cup water
1/2 cup butter or margarine

1 1/2 squares unsweetened chocolate
2 cups flour
2 cups sugar
1 teaspoon baking soda
1/2 teaspoon salt
2 eggs lightly beaten
1/2 cup sour cream
1/2 teaspoon vanilla
1 cup walnuts chopped

icing:
1/2 cup butter or margarine
1 1/2 squares unsweetendd chocolate
3 cups confectioners sugar; divide
5 tablespoons milk
1 teaspoon vanilla

## *Instructions*

In a saucepan, bring water, butter and chocolate to a boil. Boil for 1 minute. Remove from the heat; cool. In a mixing bowl, combine flour, sugar, baking soda and salt. Add eggs, sour cream and vanilla; mix. Fold in walnuts. Pour into a greased 15-inch x 10-inch x 1-inch baking pan. Bake at 350 degrees F for 20-25 minutes or until brownies test done. Cool for 10 minutes.

For icing, melt butter and chocolate. Place in a mixing bowl; mix in 1-1/2 cups confectioners sugar. Add milk, vanilla and remaining sugar; beat until smooth. Spread over warm brownies.

**Swiss Chocolate Crispies**

## *Ingredients*

1 pkg Swiss chocolate cake mix
1/2 cup butter flavor Crisco
1/2 cup butter or margarine; softened
2 eggs
2 tablespoon water
3 cups rice krispies

## Instructions

Combine cake mix, Crisco, butter, eggs, and water in large bowl. Beat at low speed with electric mixer for 2 minutes. Fold in 1 cup rice krispies cereal. Refrigerate 1 hour. Crush remaing 2 cups cereal into coarse crumbs. Preheat oven to 350°F. Grease baking sheets. Shape dough into 1-inch balls. Roll in crushed cereal. Place on baking sheets about 1 inch apart. Bake at 350°F for 11 to 13 minutes. Cool 1 minute on baking sheets. Remove to cooling rack.

**Swiss Mocha Coffee Mix**

## Ingredients

1 cup instant coffee
1 cup granulated sugar
2 cup nonfat dry milk powder
4 teaspoon cocoa powder

## Instructions

Prepare the Coffee Mix: Put all the ingredients into a blender or food processor and blend until powder consistency.

To make Swiss Mocha Coffee: In a mug, combine 2 tablespoons of creamer with 6 ounces of coffee mix.

## Swiss Mocha Mix

### *Ingredients*

1/2 cup Instant skim milk powder
2 tablespoon Cocoa
2 tablespoon Instant coffee

### *Instructions*

Combine ingredients in blender. Blend at high speed until well mixed. Or place ingredients in a jar, seal and shake.


## Swiss Noodle Bake

### *Ingredients*

1 package (12 oz) Egg Noodles, uncooked
10 oz package frozen peas, thawed and drained
2/3 cup (4 oz can) sliced mushrooms, drained
1/4 cup onion, chopped
1/2 cup butter or margarine
1/3 cup flour
1 teaspoon salt
1/2 tsp. Pepper
3 cups milk
2 cups (8 oz) shredded Swiss cheese
2 cups cooked ham, cut into 1 inch cubes
1 cup (16 oz can) tomatoes, drained and cut into small pieces

### *Instructions*

Cook egg noodles according to package directions, drain.

Melt 2 tablespoons butter or margarine in a medium saucepan. Sauté in this saucepan the peas, mushrooms and onion for 3 minutes. Remove from heat and set aside.

Melt the remaining 6 tablespoons butter or margarine in another medium saucepan. Remove it from heat. Add flour, salt and pepper and stir well. Return to heat.

Gradually add milk, stirring constantly. Cook until thickened. Add cheese. Stir until smooth and thick.

Combine egg noodles, cheese sauce, sautéed vegetables, ham cubes and tomatoes. Mix them well. Transfer into a buttered 3 quart casserole. Cover and bake at 350°F for 25-30 minutes or until bubbly.

**Swiss Nut Torte**

## *Ingredients*

3/4 cup sweet unsalted butter
2 2/3 cups flour
1 1/2 cup sugar
1 beaten egg
2 tablespoons rum or brandy
1 teaspoon grated lemon peel
1 cup heavy cream
3 tablespoons honey
2 tablespoons Kirsch
3 cups chopped walnuts (1 lb)
1 egg yolk, slightly beaten
1 tablespoon milk

## *Instructions*

Beat butter until fluffy. Gradually add 1/2 cup of the sugar. Beat well. Add egg, rum, lemon peel and flour to the butter mixture. A few drops of water may be necessary to make into a pie dough. Divide dough into thirds and pat 1/3 into the bottom of a 10 inch spring form pan. Pat another 1/3 to make the sides of the pie. Roll the remainder of the dough to 1/4 inch thick and cut into strips for the lattice on the top of the pie. Chill all for 30 minutes. In skillet melt remaining cup of sugar over low heat until golden. Remove from heat and stir in the cream. Heat and stir until sugar is dissolved. Add honey and Kirsch. Stir in nuts. Cool for 10 minutes. Spread into the dough lined pan. Pace dough strips on top of pie. Brush with beaten egg/milk mixture. Bake at 350°F for 40 minutes.

**Swiss Pudding**

*Ingredients*

1/2 cup butter
Grated rind one lemon
7/8 cup flour
5 eggs
2 cups milk
1/3 cup powdered sugar

*Instructions*

Cream the butter, add flour gradually. Scald milk with lemon rind, add to first mixture, and cook five minutes in double boiler. Beat yolks of eggs until thick and lemon-colored, add sugar gradually, then add to cooked mixture. Cool, cut and fold in whites of eggs beaten stiff.

Transfer into buttered baking form, cover, and steam one and one-fourth hours. While steaming, be sure water surrounds form to half its depth, and never reaches a lower temperature than the boiling-point.

## Miscellaneous

**Anchovy Sauce**

### *Ingredients*

6 tablespoons mayonnaise
6 tablespoons cream
8 anchovy fillet or 1 tablespoon anchovy paste
2 tablespoons chives chopped
1 teaspoon Tabasco sauce
1 teaspoon cognac or brandy

### *Instructions*

Mix mayonnaise and cream. Combine finely chopped anchovy fillet, chives, Tabasco, cognac and mayonnaise mixture and mix.

The sauce is good with all kind of meat fondue.

**Brandy Sauce #1**

### *Ingredients*

1/4 cup Butter or margarine, softened
2 cup Sifted powdered sugar
2-3 tablespoon milk

1/2 teaspoon Brandy extract

## *Instructions*

Cream butter, and gradually add powdered sugar. Add enough milk to reach desired consistency. Stir in brandy extract.

### **Brandy Sauce #2**

This is marvelous on plum pudding, fruit cake, or as a fresh fruit topping.

## *Ingredients*

3 eggs, separated
1 cup granulated sugar
2 tablespoons butter, softened
1 cup heavy cream, stiffly whipped
3 tablespoons brandy, or to taste

## *Instructions*

Beat egg yolks with sugar and butter until thick and lemon-colored. Beat egg whites until stiff but not dry, and fold into egg yolk mixture. Fold in whipped cream and add brandy.

Makes about 4 cups.

### **Chili Sauce (For Swiss Steak)**

## *Ingredients*

18 lg. tomatoes

4 onions, chopped
2 green peppers, diced
1 cup sugar
2 cup vinegar
1 teaspoon cinnamon
1/2 teaspoon cloves
2 tablespoons salt
Pepper to taste

## Instructions

Mix all and bring to a boil. Pack into pints or quarts depending on your family needs. Seal and process in boiling water bath. Very good poured over pieces of round steak and baked.

**Coffee Butter Sauce**

## Ingredients

120 g butter 60 g cream cheese 60 g hot mustard 1 teaspoon instant coffee

## Instructions

Combine butter and cream cheese. Stir until homogeneous. Add mustard and coffee. Stir. Form billet and wrap it with foil. Cool (not freeze) and slice. Serve cool.

The sauce is good with meat fondue and fish fondue.

**Curry Sauce**

## Ingredients

120 g mayonnaise
3 tablespoons milk concentrate
1 apple
1/2 onion
1-2 tablespoons curry
lemon juice to taste
salt to taste
pinch sugar

## *Instructions*

Mix the mayonnaise and the milk concentrate. Chop the apple and mix with the mayonnaise mixture. Chop finely the onion. Add it to the sauce with curry and lemon juice. Mix. Salt and pepper.

### Garlic Sauce

## *Ingredients*

4 garlic cloves
1/2 teaspoon salt
1 yolk
0.5 liter olive oil
fresh lemon juice to taste

## *Instructions*

Crush garlic with salt. Add yolk. Pour by drops the olive oil beating constantly the mixture until it becomes thick as mayonnaise. Salt and add lemon juice to taste.

The sauce is especially good with fish fondue, with fondue with asparagus and artichokes.

You may add to the sauce 3 chopped garlic cloves and/or 3 drops Tabasco.

## Geneva Sauce

### *Ingredients*

200 g concentrated fish broth
200 g red wine
2 tablespoons butter
1 cup finely chopped mushrooms
1 tablespoon chopped parsley
2-3 garlic cloves mashed
1 slice stale white bread without crust
ground black pepper
salt to taste

### *Instructions*

Preheat butter in the pan. Add mushrooms, parsley, garlic, crumbled bread, broth and red wine. Cook until the mushrooms are tender. Strain off the sauce. Salt and pepper. Serve to boiled fish.

## Marinade for Meat

### *Ingredients*

For 1 kg meat:
3/4 liter dry red wine
1 onion sliced into rings
2 carrots sliced
1 bay leaf
1 celery stem

parsley
thyme
rosemary to taste
3 peppercorns

## *Instructions*

Cut finely parsley and celery. Mix them with other ingredients and pour the marinade on meat. Place the meat in the refrigerator for 12 hours. Turn over the meat periodically.

## **Red Beet Sauce**

## *Ingredients*

1/4 sour cream
3 tablespoons beet juice
1 tablespoons lemon juice
pinch caraway
1/2 teaspoon dry dill or 1 tablespoon fresh dill
ground black pepper
salt to taste

## *Instructions*

Mix all the ingredients. Serve cooled.

The sauce is good with fat meat fondue, with herring...

## **Spinach and Swiss Chard Pasta**

## *Ingredients*

1/2 pound rotini pasta, cooked (save water)

1/4 cup pasta water
1/2 red onion, minced
3 cloves garlic, minced
1 bunch swiss chard, sliced
2 cups baby spinach, sliced
1 1/3 cups tomato pasta sauce
1 1/2 tablespoons heavy cream
1 teaspoon red pepper flakes
Olive oil
salt

## *Instructions*

1. Heat a swirl of olive oil in a pan on medium high heat and add onions and garlic. Cook until onions soften, approx. 3-5 minutes.
2. Add chard and spinach, along with pasta water and cook down until greens just begin to wilt, approx. 1-2 minutes.
3. Add pasta sauce, cream and red pepper flakes. Stir well.
4. Fold in cooked pasta until combined. Salt to taste.

Source: "Open Source Food" - opensourcefood.com.


**Swiss Asparagus Au Gratin - side dish**

## *Ingredients*

1/2 cup water
1 1/2 pounds asparagus spears - trimmed
2 ounces finely shredded natural Swiss cheese
1/4 cup dry bread crumbs
2 tablespoons kraft touch of butter spread - melted
1/2 teaspoon dry mustard
1/8 teaspoon pepper

## Instructions

Preheat the oven to 400°F. Bring 1/2 cup water to boil in a skillet. Add asparagus. Cook for 2 minutes. Drain.

Place in a 10 x 6 inch baking dish. Mix remaining ingredients and sprinkle over asparagus. Bake for 8 to 10 minutes or until the cheese mixture is lightly browned.


**Swiss Broccoli Pasta**

## Ingredients

28 ounces broccoli cuts
8 ounces margarine - melted
8 ounces all-purpose flour
3 1/4 quarts milk
52 ounces Swiss cheese - shredded
1/4 teaspoon ground nutmeg
1 pound canned sliced mushrooms - drained
5 pounds pasta
5 gallons boiling water
5 ounces salt
3 tablespoons vegetable oil

## Instructions

Prepare sauce:
Steam broccoli until tender. Drain. Combine margarine and flour in a kettle. Stir and cook for 5-10 minutes until smooth. Add milk gradually. Stirring constantly, cook over low heat until thick. Remove from heat. Add cheese and stir until melted. Stir in nutmeg. Stir in mushrooms and broccoli. Keep hot: 180°F (80°C). The sauce is ready.

Cook pasta. Drain.

Serve 4 oz sauce over 4 oz pasta. Thin sauce as necessary with hot milk.

**Swiss Sauced Broccoli - side dish**

## *Ingredients*

6 ounces fresh broccoli
2 tablespoons water
1/8 teaspoon salt
2 teaspoons butter or margarine
1 1/2 teaspoons unbleached flour
pinch of salt
pinch of white pepper
1/3 cup milk
1/4 cup shredded Swiss cheese

## *Instructions*

Wash broccoli. Remove outer leaves and tough part of stalks. Cut stalks lengthwise into uniform spears, following the branching lines. In a 1-quart casserole combine broccoli, water and 1/8 teaspoon salt. Cover the casserole and cook in microwave oven at 100% power for 5 to 6 minutes or just till tender. Let it stand, covered, while you prepare the sauce.

Prepare the sauce in an uncovered 1-cup measure micro-cook butter or margarine at 100% power for 30 to 45 seconds or until melted. Add in flour, salt and pepper. Stir. Pour milk. Stir. Micro-cook, uncovered, at 100% power for 1 to 2 minutes or until thickened and bubbly, stirring every 30 seconds. Add shredded Swiss cheese. Wait until it melts.

Drain Broccoli. Serve sauce over broccoli.


## Swiss Style Green Beans - site dish

### *Ingredients*

2 tablespoons Grated Onion
7 tablespoons Margarine
2 tablespoons Sugar
1 tablespoon Salt
1 tablespoon White Pepper
1 Pint Sour Cream
8 oz Grated Swiss Cheese
4 16 oz Cans-French Style Green Beans
1/2 Cup Crushed Corn Flakes

### *Instructions*

Saute the onions in 4 tablespoons of the margarine. Add the flour, sugar, salt and white pepper. Mix well. Add the sour cream. Stir. Cook until thick, stirring occasionally. Drain the green beans and add to the sour cream mixture.

Pour into a buttered casserole. Top with Swiss cheese. Melt the remaining 3 tablespoons of margarine, then stir in the corn flakes. Spread over the top of the cheese. Bake at 350°F for 30-40 minutes.


## Tomato Sauce

### *Ingredients*

1 tomato
1/4 teaspoon dry tarragon

2 tablespoons tomato paste
4 drops Tabasco sauce
125 g mayonnaise

## *Instructions*

Peel tomato and remove seeds. Chop fine. Mix with other ingredients.

The sauce is good with fondue with asparagus or artichoke.

Printed in Great Britain
by Amazon.co.uk, Ltd.,
Marston Gate.